GODDESS in motion

An inspirational avtivity book to awaken the Goddess within! Join Belly-Dance Superstar Nadirah and Friends as they dance around the world spreading health an well-being to all.

By Nadirah R. Bray
&
Christina Fumiko Barrows

To: Jack, Benjamin and Henry

You are my son, my moon, my stars.
You are precious in every way.
The sunshine in my day.
The joy in my soul and the love of my life.
Love Ma, Rae, Raemole
          Mom

Lesa,
Thank you for
your Beautiful heart!
I love you! Let your inner
Goddess shine every day and
in every way!
♡
Nadiroh

The Healing Power of Dance!

The physical benefits of belly dance include evenly strengthening your core and spine, thus promoting great posture. This ancient art form Increases muscle tone and flexibility, which allows you builds a stronger body from the inside out. The faster movements are great for your cardiovascular system, increasing blood flow and promoting the flow of oxygen throughout the body. The slower movements elevate you self awareness and muscle control, and evenly become a form of meditation. The movements are low impact, which is gentle on your back and joints. Dance helps clear the mind and allows you to let go of stress easily.

The mental benefits include building new neural pathways, enhance compassion and empathy , a sense of empowerment, relaxation, quite your mind and increase your creativity.

The emotional benefits increase your self-esteem, allow you to effortlessly express your passions,contentment, happiness, fulfill-ment , and feeling of accomplishment.

The spiritual benefits are feeling centered, grounded, and connect-ed to your self, others and your higher power. Let belly dance and sensual experiential movement exercise your body, relax your mind and lift your spirits.

Nadirah

I am Worthy

You are made of stardust,
shine like the goddess you are.
    —Nadirah

Benefits of Bellydance

Releases endorphins which Provide natural pain relief

Increase self-esteem

Promote positive body image

Burns at least 445 cal an hour

Reduces stress, anxiety and depression

Improved heart function

Boosts memory

Lift your spirits

Better balance

Conditions the abdominal muscles

Immune system booster

Helps move nutrients and oxygen throughout the body

Improves happiness and social connection

Connect you to your creativity

Stronger bones that reduce risk of osteoporosis

What one has not experienced,
one will never understand in print.
-Isadora Duncan

All I want is to be happy, so I dance!

Adira

If you can't control it, let it go.

"If you love living, you try to take care of the equipment."
    -Sally Rand

THE DANCE IS A POEM OF WHICH
EACH MOVEMENT IS A WORD."
                    -MATA HARI

Until you spread your wings, you'll have no idea how far you can fly.

Ariel   Lynda   Arista

Give your stress wings
and let it fly away
                    -Terri Guillemets

"I must be a mermaid, I have no fear of depths and a great fear of shallow living."
-Anaïs Nin

Vegetables Word Search

Search the puzzle for the words shown in the word list. Circle each word that you find until you find all of the 24 vegetable-related words.

Word List

brussels sprouts

potato	cucumber
pumpkin	lettuce
alfalfa	parsley
artichoke	pepper
asparagus	rhubarb
avocado	carrot
broccoli	radish
cabbage	beans
cauliflower	spinach
celery	zucchini
corn	yam
	pea

```
Y A M B R O C C O L I R B A G
C A U L I F L O W E R D Q L P
C U C U M B E R N Z T T C F A
Y Y N S P I N A C H S J O A R
Z R O A E C A B B A G E R L S
M Z O R A D I S H M V B N F L
K A A S P A R A G U S G X A E
R F A Q M B P U M P K I N Y Y
B R U S S E L S S P R O U T S
C Q O P N A L E T T U C E L M
E K G O S N A R T I C H O K E
L O U T I S R H U B A R B D T
E B F A L Y Z U C C H I N I H
R J V T C A R R O T T N E F F
Y A V O C A D O G P E P P E R
```

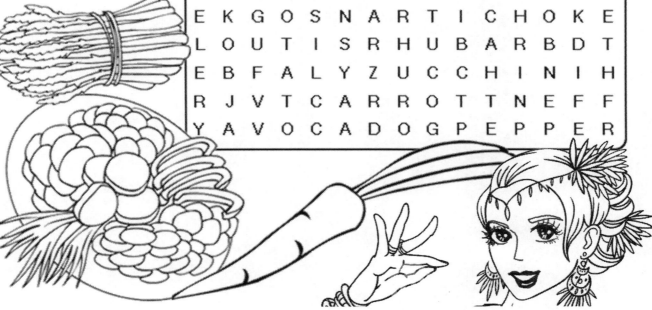

Let your Spirit Soar

There is no magic step that makes you a great dancer, there is only the magic you put in each and every step."
- FAHTIEM

*We are all of us unique - each a unique pattern of cre-
ativity and if we do not fufill it, it is lost real time.*
                              -Maths Graham

Labyrinths are based on ancient patterns and thought to hold meditative powers. Walking a labyrinth promotes healing and mindfulness

ALL ABOUT

I am ◯ years old

I Live with

My Friends Are

in

I like to watch

Favorite activities

My Favorite:

COLOR:_____

FOOD:_____

ANIMAL:_____

BOOKS:

I am good at

When I grow up
I want to be...

Made in the USA
San Bernardino, CA
20 May 2018

HOME

Written by Lindsay Bednar

Illustrated by Ira Baykovska

Rodney K Press
Minneapolis, MN

Home
A Kozy Nook Book
Published by Rodney K Press
www.rodneykpress.com
info@rodneykpress.com
Minneapolis, MN

Library of Congress Control Number: 2017934251
Bednar, Lindsay Author
Baykovska, Ira Illustrator
Home

ISBN: 978-0-9984480-1-5

JUVENILE FICTION / Imagination & Play
JUVENILE FICTION / Stories in Verse

For our children,
Whitney and Garrison,
for making our house a home.

For my Mom and Grandpa Rodney
for being my constant inspirations.

And to my husband—thank you
for encouraging me to leap.

Home is the place
where imagination takes shape

Where crowns are adorned
and heroes wear capes

Where tickles and giggles
can always be found

Where forts are constructed

and knocked to the ground.

Where paintings and drawings
can cover the walls

And plays are presented
on stages in halls.

Where music and instruments
beg to be played

And dances
and silliest of songs can be made.

Home
is the place
where

we grow
and
we learn

Where mistakes
are okay

and we wait
for our turn.

Where potty is practiced
with charts and with cheers
And tantrums bring timeouts
and wiped away tears.

Where batter is stirred
and cupcakes are baked

And patience is practiced
while cooling takes place.

Where temps will be taken
for sickness and bugs
And tempers are calmed
with a kiss and a hug.

Home is the place
where we feel safe and sound

Where comfort and cozy
can always be found.

Where toddlers are sung to
and held while they're swayed

And babies fall gently asleep
where they're laid.

Where baths leave us clean and
teeth are all brushed

And flashlights and nightlights
help fears to be hushed.

It's where all of us snuggle
and read every night

Where fantasies, hopes,
and dreams can take flight.

Home is the place
Where we all become one

Where there's cuddles
and kisses and all sorts of fun!

About the Author

Lindsay Bednar is a mom, a wife, a daughter, a sister, a movie-quoter and a freestyle rap enthusiast. She has spent much of her career teaching high school English and working with at-risk students. From the city of St. Paul, MN to the small town of Princeton, Lindsay has loved connecting with and working with teens.

Lindsay's life changed when asked this deceptively simple question: what does home mean to you? Considering this question inspired Lindsay's first book, *Home*, and motivated her to leave teaching to spend more time with her children and pursue writing. *Home* led to the creation of A Kozy Nook Book series, in which she poignantly depicts the good feels that come with some of her favorite corners of the world.

Lindsay lives just outside of Minneapolis, MN with her husband, two children and giant Newfoundland, Grizz.

Visit Lindsay's website at www.lindsaybednar.com.

About the Illustrator

Ira Baykovska's career began with doodles in her mother's recipe books when she was three years old. From there she moved to drawing on the walls in her bedroom and then to the many notepads that she made into her own books.

Now in her twenties, Ira has discovered what she really wants to do with her life. She loves to illustrate books for children and has created fifteen children's books. It always amazes her how words on paper become real in colors and lines.

Ira has a degree in Graphic Design from Ukrainian Academy in Printing and is based in Lviv, Ukraine.

Made in United States
Orlando, FL
09 June 2022